Flex Your FAITH Planner

Nikki Pinkney

Ezekiel Family Services

DEDICATION

This is dedicated to all the people out there who dare to believe God! The bible says in Habakkuk 2:2 (AMP) to write the vision and make it plain upon tablets, so that the one who reads it can run with it. The practice of writing down what you are believing God for from what you believe he is revealing to you and recording the manifestations of this insight is flexing your FAITH. In this planner you will write down your revelations of Faith daily, mark them with the date and time in the morning, then you will come back before bed and record the time and your reflections from the day. This creates an ongoing plan, vision, and history of how God is moving in your life and when you need strength to believe for something else you have your personal record of Faith experiences with God. *Flex your Faith Planner* is you planning your future based on what you believe God is showing you, taking the risk to believe what you don't see yet, and putting action to it as if God has already made it your reality. This planner is your future fulfilled and a written history of your Faith.

"Now FAITH is the substance of things hoped for, the evidence of things not seen." (Hebrews 11:1 NKJV). Make a monument of your FAITH. Faith is the currency of the kingdom of God. God manifests his promises based upon FAITH. Our FAITH motivates him to move. The people in the bible created monuments when God fulfilled his promise to them. We have to learn to document our Faith moments with God. The things God puts in our hearts, the things God inspires us to do, and the things we believe he will do in our lives. This Faith planner creates a tangible way to track the way God does things in your life personally.

We all have a personal journey of Faith we have taken with God. We may not have always documented these experiences. My family has been an instrumental part of my Faith journey and a tool like this planner to help me strategically identify God's activity in my life would have been a great access in my earlier years with God.

This planner will help you identify the voice of God, see your future through God's eyes, learn the nature of God and how the kingdom shows up in your life. The planner will also help you to develop unmovable Faith. No matter what you are facing you will have Faith like Abraham when he had to sacrifice Isaac to obey God, with the assurance that God was going to provide a ram in the bush. This Faith planner will give you the assurance that what God asks you to do, he has already gone before you to make sure the manifestation of his promise will prevail. The table of contents is designed for you to write the topic you are exercising your Faith for that day. This planner is designed for you to strengthen your Faith and awareness of how the Holy Spirit speaks personally to you and operates in your life.

So, buckle your seat belt and get ready to see things you've never discovered or heard before, things beyond your ability to imagine. God has in store to reveal to you things no eyes have seen and no ears have heard, and to show you your future the way he sees it. Create the space for God to surpass your human logic and take you into the kingdom of God and the way he sees life.

He will take you into the supernatural realms and give you experiences with him to document in the *FLEX YOUR FAITH PLANNER* that will shape your relationship with him for life.

TABLE OF CONTENTS

(Write your Faith topic for each day)

Faith Flexor 1 ______________________________

Faith Flexor 2 ______________________________

Faith Flexor 3 ______________________________

Faith Flexor 4 ______________________________

Faith Flexor 5 ______________________________

Faith Flexor 6 ______________________________

Faith Flexor 7 ______________________________

Faith Flexor 8 ______________________________

Faith Flexor 9 ______________________________

Faith Flexor 10 ______________________________

Faith Flexor 11 ______________________________

Faith Flexor 12 ______________________________

Faith Flexor 13 ______________________________

Faith Flexor 14 ______________________________

Faith Flexor 15 ______________________________

Faith Flexor 16

Faith Flexor 17

Faith Flexor 18

Faith Flexor 19

Faith Flexor 20

Faith Flexor 21

Faith Flexor 22

Faith Flexor 23

Faith Flexor 24

Faith Flexor 25

Faith Flexor 26

Faith Flexor 27

Faith Flexor 28

Faith Flexor 29

Faith Flexor 30

Faith Flexor 31

INTRODUCTION

The idea to write this book came while coaching one of my clients one evening. I was telling her for the week to write down everything she is believing God for. Then as the week goes on, mark off everything that God does. I was guiding her how to see God in her life to strengthen her trust and history with God. When I was done giving her this assignment she said, "Wait, this can be a planner you make for people to document their Faith journey with God as they learn how to see God in their lives." I pondered on it for a moment and said, "Okay, I will pray on it."

To be honest, I did not start writing when she first presented the idea because I had to wait for the Holy Spirit to inspire it in me. I have learned a good idea is not always God. In my waiting, I began to pay attention to the way God was speaking to me and what he wanted me to pay attention to or what he was making me aware of. I do this when I am awaiting the way God will respond to something I present to him. This makes me sensitive to the way he is communicating with me. I also look at my life and current lessons God is teaching me and see if it aligns with the thought or desire I am putting before him.

The things I was experiencing were causing me to flex my Faith through self-expression before I was inspired to write the book. I always believe God has us do a thing behind the scenes with him before he releases it to the public to see or encounter. He is testing the integrity of our hearts and character. He wants to know if we are doing it for the fame and approval of people or for him. When it prospers will we take the credit or give him the glory? This is so important to the kingdom of God. Anything God births in us is for the people's benefit and for his glory. It is always to draw man unto him. It is always to show man how great he is and our need for him.

God does this because we live in a world that wants to remove God out of everything. It wants to give the universe credit for things God created. The universe was created to conform to what we command it to do; we were not created to be ruled by, nor look for answers from the universe. This is why I believe God gave me the yes to write this *Flex Your Faith Planner* for the purpose of helping you see him in everything, look to him for answers, and to let you know you have the power to use words to command the universe to yield to the God in you! In Gen. 2:19 (New King James Version) it says, "Out of the ground the Lord God formed every beast of the field and every bird of the air and brought them to Adam to see what he would call them. And whatever Adam called each living creature, that was its name." GOD BROUGHT THE ANIMALS TO ADAM TO SEE WHAT HE WOULD CALL THEM. God gave Adam permission to name the animals. He did not look to the universe to name the animals. We must remember God is our source and everything else on this earth is a resource that God gives us the power and authority to rule so we can live life on this earth in the fullness of who he called us to be for his glory.

As you start your Faith journey with God in this planner, keep in mind that you are on a journey of discovering how to *FLEX YOUR FAITH* so when God through the Holy Spirit comes to you and says, "What do you want to call this?" "What do you want this to do?" "How do you want me to move?" you are ready to respond according to his plans, purposes, and promises revealed to you because you have a record of how you FLEXED YOUR FAITH and GOD delivered!

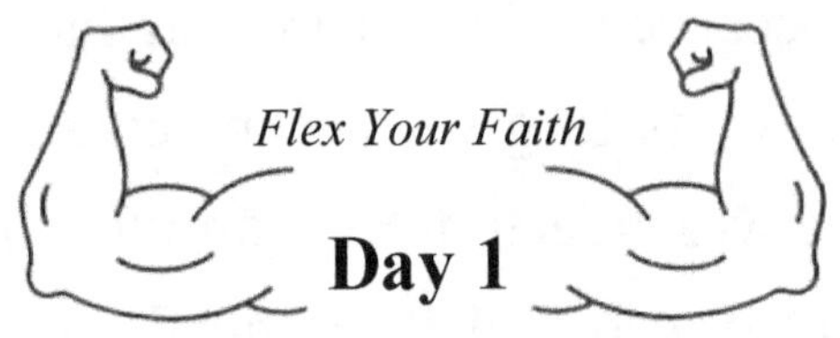

Faith Prayer

By Faith, peace and clarity are cultivated as you write in this planner and release your Faith.

Date:

Time:

What are you believing God for today?

Write a scripture that you can stand on that aligns with your Faith today.

What do you expect God to do based on your belief today?

Time:

Did you see any manifestation today of what you put your Faith towards?

If yes, what did you see?

How did God show himself (through his word, dream or vision, peace, circumstance, nature, divine impression, audible voice, or other)?

If nothing was revealed, what did you discover new today and how did you see God in your day?

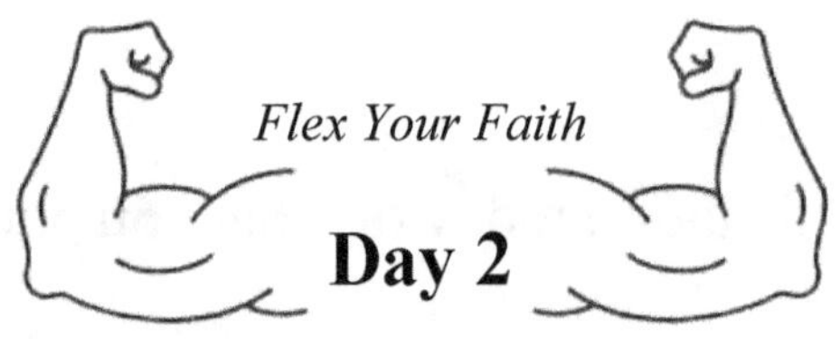

Day 2

Faith Prayer

By Faith, creativity and imagination will guide you as you believe God today.

Date:

Time:

What are you believing God for today?

Write a scripture that you can stand on that aligns with your Faith today.

What do you expect God to do based on your belief today?

Time:

Did you see any manifestation today of what you put your Faith towards?

If yes, what did you see?

How did God show himself (through his word, dream or vision, peace, circumstance, nature, divine impression, audible voice, or other)?

If nothing was revealed, what did you discover new today and how did you see God in your day?

Day 3

Faith Prayer

By Faith, fear will not stop you from dreaming big and trusting God today.

Date:

Time:

What are you believing God for today?

Write a scripture that you can stand on that aligns with your Faith today.

What do you expect God to do based on your belief today?

Time:

Did you see any manifestation today of what you put your Faith towards?

If yes, what did you see?

How did God show himself (through his word, dream or vision, peace, circumstance, nature, divine impression, audible voice, or other)?

If nothing was revealed, what did you discover new today and how did you see God in your day?

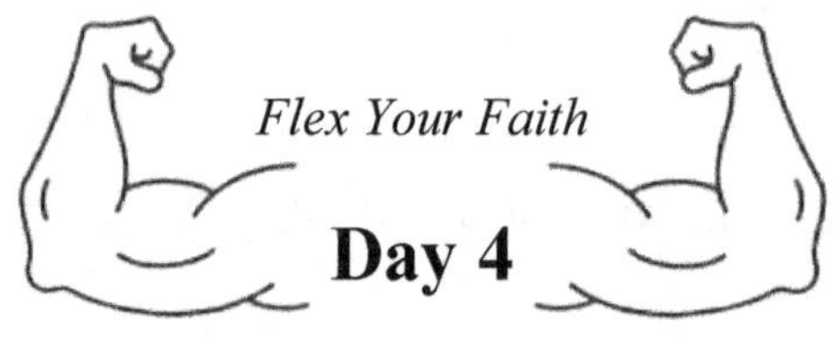

Faith Prayer

By Faith, you have heightened gratitude.

Date:

Time:

What are you believing God for today?

Write a scripture that you can stand on that aligns with your Faith today.

What do you expect God to do based on your belief today?

Time:

Did you see any manifestation today of what you put your Faith towards?

If yes, what did you see?

How did God show himself (through his word, dream or vision, peace, circumstance, nature, divine impression, audible voice, or other)?

If nothing was revealed, what did you discover new today and how did you see God in your day?

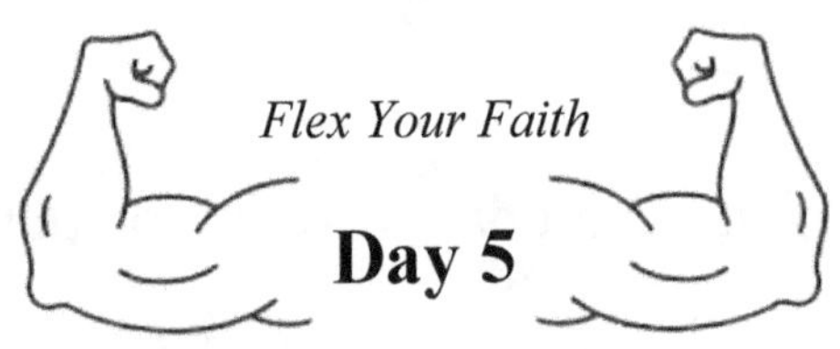

Faith Prayer

By Faith, your Faith is ignited, and you will take more risks.

Date:

Time:

What are you believing God for today?

Write a scripture that you can stand on that aligns with your Faith today.

What do you expect God to do based on your belief today?

Time:

Did you see any manifestation today of what you put your Faith towards?

If yes, what did you see?

How did God show himself (through his word, dream or vision, peace, circumstance, nature, divine impression, audible voice, or other)?

If nothing was revealed, what did you discover new today and how did you see God in your day?

Faith Prayer

By Faith, your curiosity of God is increased and will open your eyes to see him in new ways.

Date:

Time:

What are you believing God for today?

Write a scripture that you can stand on that aligns with your Faith today.

What do you expect God to do based on your belief today?

Time:

Did you see any manifestation today of what you put your Faith towards?

If yes, what did you see?

How did God show himself (through his word, dream or vision, peace, circumstance, nature, divine impression, audible voice, or other)?

If nothing was revealed, what did you discover new today and how did you see God in your day?

Faith Prayer

By Faith, today you will write from your heart with no reservations.

Date:

Time:

What are you believing God for today?

Write a scripture that you can stand on that aligns with your Faith today.

What do you expect God to do based on your belief today?

Time:

Did you see any manifestation today of what you put your Faith towards?

If yes, what did you see?

How did God show himself (through his word, dream or vision, peace, circumstance, nature, divine impression, audible voice, or other)?

If nothing was revealed, what did you discover new today and how did you see God in your day?

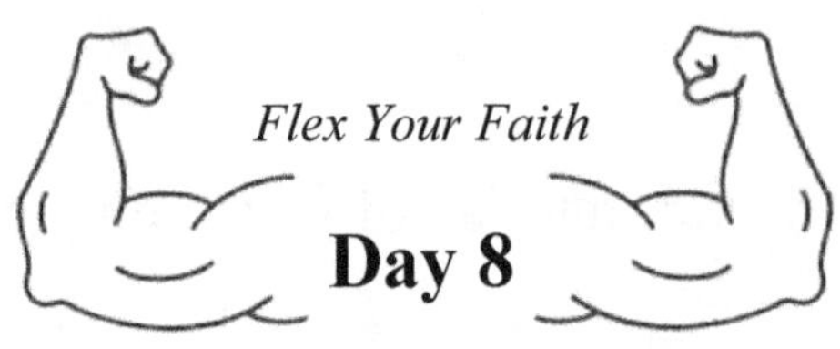

Faith Prayer

By Faith, your belief in God's power outweighs the flaws you believe about yourself.

Date:

Time:

What are you believing God for today?

Write a scripture that you can stand on that aligns with your Faith today.

What do you expect God to do based on your belief today?

Time:

Did you see any manifestation today of what you put your Faith towards?

If yes, what did you see?

How did God show himself (through his word, dream or vision, peace, circumstance, nature, divine impression, audible voice, or other)?

If nothing was revealed, what did you discover new today and how did you see God in your day?

Day 9

Faith Prayer

By Faith, God reveals to you he was always with you in memories of trauma.

Date:

Time:

What are you believing God for today?

Write a scripture that you can stand on that aligns with your Faith today.

What do you expect God to do based on your belief today?

Time:

Did you see any manifestation today of what you put your Faith towards?

If yes, what did you see?

How did God show himself (through his word, dream or vision, peace, circumstance, nature, divine impression, audible voice, or other)?

If nothing was revealed, what did you discover new today and how did you see God in your day?

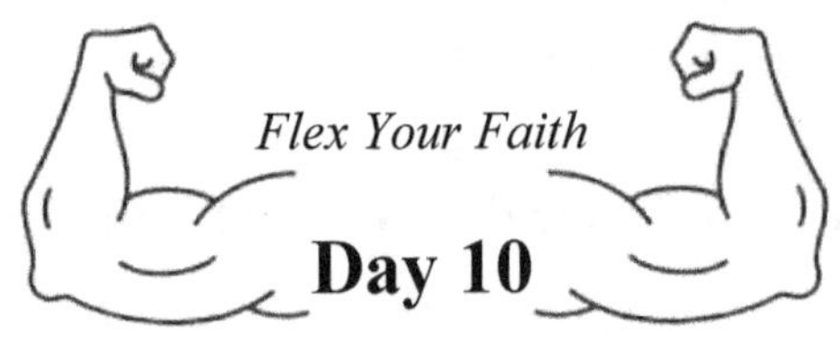

Faith Prayer

By Faith, you dare to believe in areas you have protected yourself from God and people.

Date:

Time:

What are you believing God for today?

Write a scripture that you can stand on that aligns with your Faith today.

What do you expect God to do based on your belief today?

Time:

Did you see any manifestation today of what you put your Faith towards?

If yes, what did you see?

How did God show himself (through his word, dream or vision, peace, circumstance, nature, divine impression, audible voice, or other)?

If nothing was revealed, what did you discover new today and how did you see God in your day?

Day 11

Faith Prayer

By Faith, you will face the fears that are blocking your vulnerability to believe God.

Date:

Time:

What are you believing God for today?

Write a scripture that you can stand on that aligns with your Faith today.

What do you expect God to do based on your belief today?

Time:

Did you see any manifestation today of what you put your Faith towards?

If yes, what did you see?

How did God show himself (through his word, dream or vision, peace, circumstance, nature, divine impression, audible voice, or other)?

If nothing was revealed, what did you discover new today and how did you see God in your day?

Faith Prayer

By Faith, you have courage to believe God.

Date:

Time:

What are you believing God for today?

Write a scripture that you can stand on that aligns with your Faith today.

What do you expect God to do based on your belief today?

Time:

Did you see any manifestation today of what you put your Faith towards?

If yes, what did you see?

How did God show himself (through his word, dream or vision, peace, circumstance, nature, divine impression, audible voice, or other)?

If nothing was revealed, what did you discover new today and how did you see God in your day?

Day 13

Faith Prayer

By Faith, you will turn your heart towards God when you feel justified not to trust him.

Date:

Time:

What are you believing God for today?

Write a scripture that you can stand on that aligns with your Faith today.

What do you expect God to do based on your belief today?

Time:

Did you see any manifestation today of what you put your Faith towards?

If yes, what did you see?

How did God show himself (through his word, dream or vision, peace, circumstance, nature, divine impression, audible voice, or other)?

If nothing was revealed, what did you discover new today and how did you see God in your day?

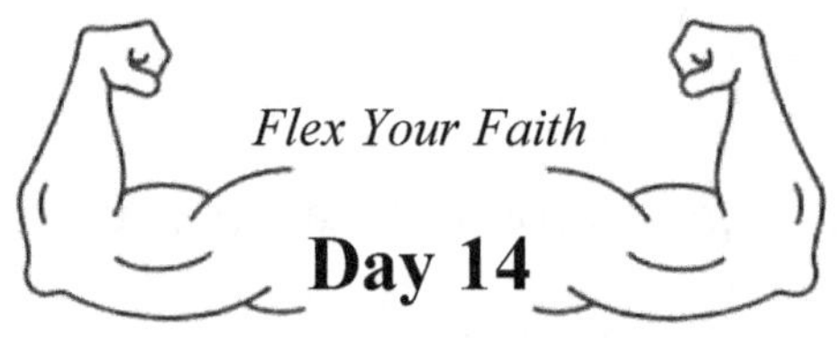

Faith Prayer

By Faith, today you will let yourself off the hook and allow God to love you.

Date:

Time:

What are you believing God for today?

Write a scripture that you can stand on that aligns with your Faith today.

What do you expect God to do based on your belief today?

Time:

Did you see any manifestation today of what you put your Faith towards?

If yes, what did you see?

How did God show himself (through his word, dream or vision, peace, circumstance, nature, divine impression, audible voice, or other)?

If nothing was revealed, what did you discover new today and how did you see God in your day?

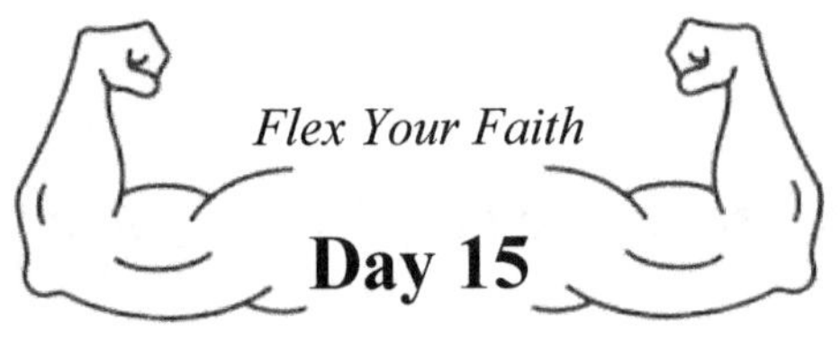

Faith Prayer

By Faith, you will receive God's help today.

Date:

Time:

What are you believing God for today?

Write a scripture that you can stand on that aligns with your Faith today.

What do you expect God to do based on your belief today?

Time:

Did you see any manifestation today of what you put your Faith towards?

If yes, what did you see?

How did God show himself (through his word, dream or vision, peace, circumstance, nature, divine impression, audible voice, or other)?

If nothing was revealed, what did you discover new today and how did you see God in your day?

Faith Prayer

By Faith, you will release everyone who has hurt you and forgive them.

Date:

Time:

What are you believing God for today?

Write a scripture that you can stand on that aligns with your Faith today.

What do you expect God to do based on your belief today?

Time:

Did you see any manifestation today of what you put your Faith towards?

If yes, what did you see?

How did God show himself (through his word, dream or vision, peace, circumstance, nature, divine impression, audible voice, or other)?

If nothing was revealed, what did you discover new today and how did you see God in your day?

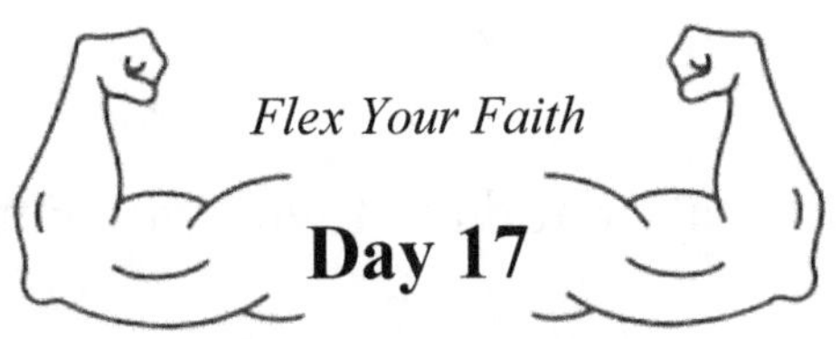

Faith Prayer

By Faith, your eyes will be opened to God's Faithfulness.

Date:

Time:

What are you believing God for today?

Write a scripture that you can stand on that aligns with your Faith today.

What do you expect God to do based on your belief today?

Time:

Did you see any manifestation today of what you put your Faith towards?

If yes, what did you see?

How did God show himself (through his word, dream or vision, peace, circumstance, nature, divine impression, audible voice, or other)?

If nothing was revealed, what did you discover new today and how did you see God in your day?

Faith Prayer

By Faith, you depend on God to birth new ways of believing him today.

Date:

Time:

What are you believing God for today?

Write a scripture that you can stand on that aligns with your Faith today.

What do you expect God to do based on your belief today?

Time:

Did you see any manifestation today of what you put your Faith towards?

If yes, what did you see?

How did God show himself (through his word, dream or vision, peace, circumstance, nature, divine impression, audible voice, or other)?

If nothing was revealed, what did you discover new today and how did you see God in your day?

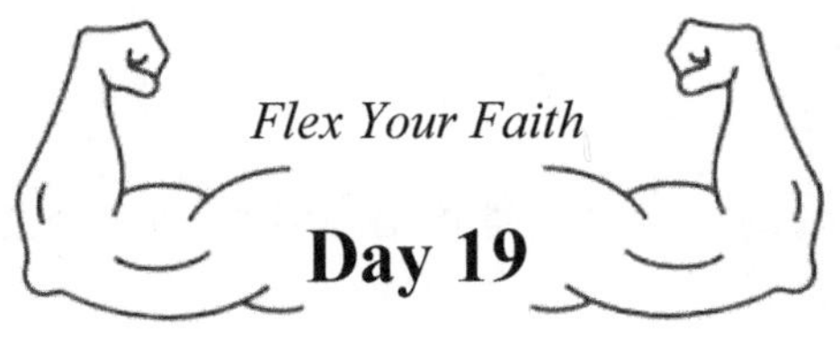

Faith Prayer

By Faith, there is no limit to what God will reveal to you.

Date:

Time:

What are you believing God for today?

Write a scripture that you can stand on that aligns with your Faith today.

What do you expect God to do based on your belief today?

Time:

Did you see any manifestation today of what you put your Faith towards?

If yes, what did you see?

How did God show himself (through his word, dream or vision, peace, circumstance, nature, divine impression, audible voice, or other)?

If nothing was revealed, what did you discover new today and how did you see God in your day?

Faith Prayer

By Faith, God is strengthening you in him.

Date:

Time:

What are you believing God for today?

Write a scripture that you can stand on that aligns with your Faith today.

What do you expect God to do based on your belief today?

Time:

Did you see any manifestation today of what you put your Faith towards?

If yes, what did you see?

How did God show himself (through his word, dream or vision, peace, circumstance, nature, divine impression, audible voice, or other)?

If nothing was revealed, what did you discover new today and how did you see God in your day?

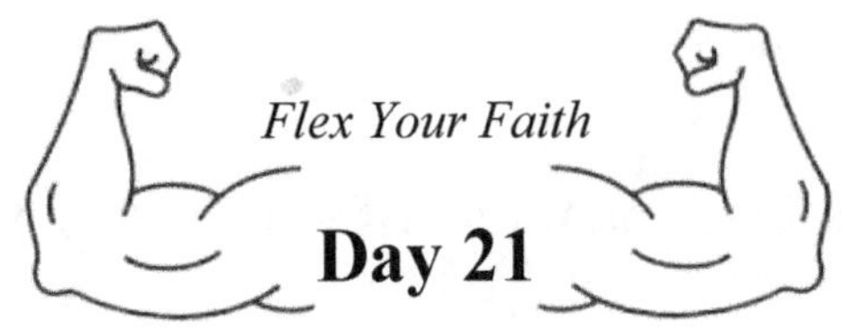

Faith Prayer

By Faith, God is filling you up with the fullness of his spirit.

Date:

Time:

What are you believing God for today?

Write a scripture that you can stand on that aligns with your Faith today.

What do you expect God to do based on your belief today?

Time:

Did you see any manifestation today of what you put your Faith towards?

If yes, what did you see?

How did God show himself (through his word, dream or vision, peace, circumstance, nature, divine impression, audible voice, or other)?

If nothing was revealed, what did you discover new today and how did you see God in your day?

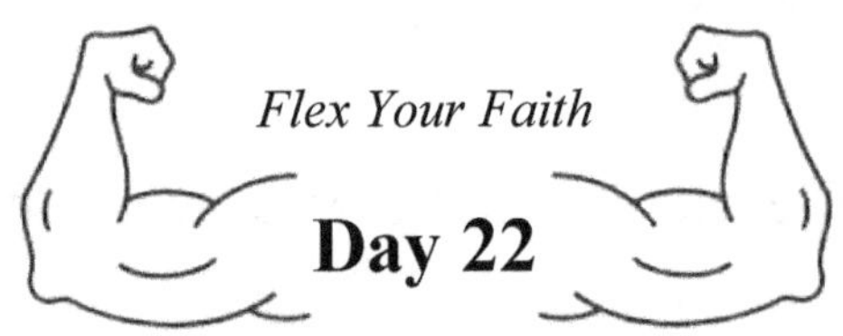

Faith Prayer

By Faith, God is breaking every stronghold off your mind, will, and emotions.

Date:

Time:

What are you believing God for today?

Write a scripture that you can stand on that aligns with your Faith today.

What do you expect God to do based on your belief today?

Time:

Did you see any manifestation today of what you put your Faith towards?

If yes, what did you see?

How did God show himself (through his word, dream or vision, peace, circumstance, nature, divine impression, audible voice, or other)?

If nothing was revealed, what did you discover new today and how did you see God in your day?

Faith Prayer

By Faith, God is changing old things to new.

Date:

Time:

What are you believing God for today?

Write a scripture that you can stand on that aligns with your Faith today.

What do you expect God to do based on your belief today?

Time:

Did you see any manifestation today of what you put your Faith towards?

If yes, what did you see?

How did God show himself (through his word, dream or vision, peace, circumstance, nature, divine impression, audible voice, or other)?

If nothing was revealed, what did you discover new today and how did you see God in your day?

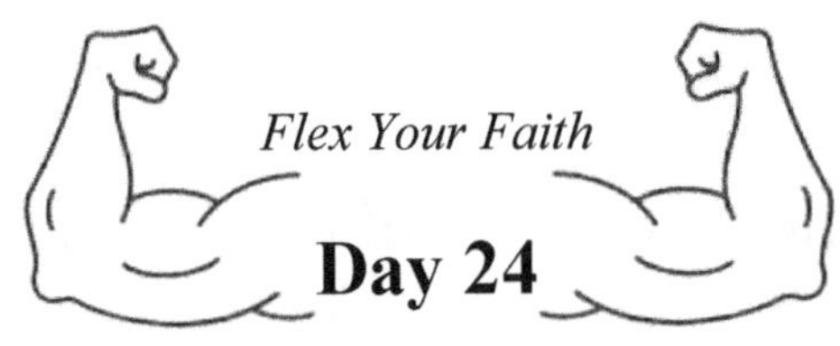

Faith Prayer

By Faith, you will discover divine secrets that will advance you in your purpose.

Date:

Time:

What are you believing God for today?

Write a scripture that you can stand on that aligns with your Faith today.

What do you expect God to do based on your belief today?

Time:

Did you see any manifestation today of what you put your Faith towards?

If yes, what did you see?

How did God show himself (through his word, dream or vision, peace, circumstance, nature, divine impression, audible voice, or other)?

If nothing was revealed, what did you discover new today and how did you see God in your day?

Day 25

Faith Prayer

By Faith, the Holy Spirit is purging your life of any mindsets that are disempowering you.

Date:

Time:

What are you believing God for today?

Write a scripture that you can stand on that aligns with your Faith today.

What do you expect God to do based on your belief today?

Time:

Did you see any manifestation today of what you put your Faith towards?

57 | Page

If yes, what did you see?

How did God show himself (through his word, dream or vision, peace, circumstance, nature, divine impression, audible voice, or other)?

If nothing was revealed, what did you discover new today and how did you see God in your day?

Day 26

Faith Prayer

By Faith, you are being led into relationships that will evolve and mature you in Christ.

Date:

Time:

What are you believing God for today?

Write a scripture that you can stand on that aligns with your Faith today.

What do you expect God to do based on your belief today?

Time:

Did you see any manifestation today of what you put your Faith towards?

If yes, what did you see?

How did God show himself (through his word, dream or vision, peace, circumstance, nature, divine impression, audible voice, or other)?

If nothing was revealed, what did you discover new today and how did you see God in your day?

Faith Prayer

By Faith, increase in every area of your life that has experienced lack.

Date:

Time:

What are you believing God for today?

Write a scripture that you can stand on that aligns with your Faith today.

What do you expect God to do based on your belief today?

Time:

Did you see any manifestation today of what you put your Faith towards?

If yes, what did you see?

How did God show himself (through his word, dream or vision, peace, circumstance, nature, divine impression, audible voice, or other)?

If nothing was revealed, what did you discover new today and how did you see God in your day?

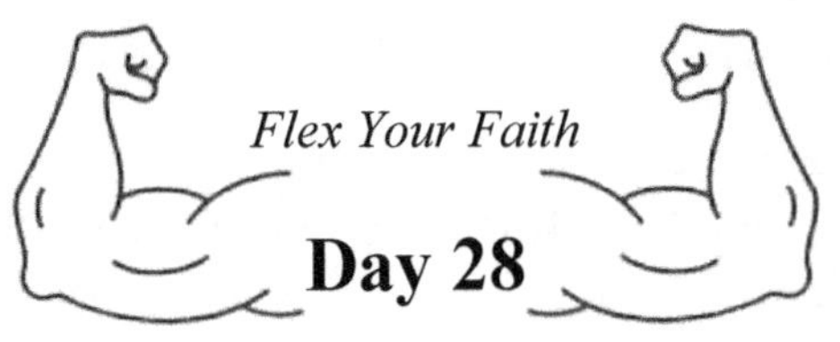

Faith Prayer

By Faith, expect miracles to take place right before your eyes.

Date:

Time:

What are you believing God for today?

Write a scripture that you can stand on that aligns with your Faith today.

What do you expect God to do based on your belief today?

Time:

Did you see any manifestation today of what you put your Faith towards?

If yes, what did you see?

How did God show himself (through his word, dream or vision, peace, circumstance, nature, divine impression, audible voice, or other)?

If nothing was revealed, what did you discover new today and how did you see God in your day?

Faith Prayer

By Faith, unexpected income will manifest in your life.

Date:

Time:

What are you believing God for today?

Write a scripture that you can stand on that aligns with your Faith today.

What do you expect God to do based on your belief today?

Time:

Did you see any manifestation today of what you put your Faith towards?

If yes, what did you see?

How did God show himself (through his word, dream or vision, peace, circumstance, nature, divine impression, audible voice, or other)?

If nothing was revealed, what did you discover new today and how did you see God in your day?

Faith Prayer
By Faith, supernatural healing is all around you.

Date:

Time:

What are you believing God for today?

Write a scripture that you can stand on that aligns with your Faith today.

What do you expect God to do based on your belief today?

Time:

Did you see any manifestation today of what you put your Faith towards?

67 | Page

If yes, what did you see?

How did God show himself (through his word, dream or vision, peace, circumstance, nature, divine impression, audible voice, or other)?

If nothing was revealed, what did you discover new today and how did you see God in your day?

Day 31

Faith Prayer

By Faith, your Faith has been strengthened and you're ready to "Flex your FAITH."

Date:

Time:

What are you believing God for today?

Write a scripture that you can stand on that aligns with your Faith today.

What do you expect God to do based on your belief today?

Time:

Did you see any manifestation today of what you put your Faith towards?

If yes, what did you see?

How did God show himself (through his word, dream or vision, peace, circumstance, nature, divine impression, audible voice, or other)?

If nothing was revealed, what did you discover new today and how did you see God in your day?

ADDITIONAL PAGES TO JOURNAL FAITH THOUGHTS

ADDITIONAL JOURNAL PAGES

71 | Page

REFLECTION

Faith without works is dead. Our actions have to align with our Faith. The Holy Spirit told me FAITH is **Facts As In The Heavens**. When the Holy Spirit reveals to us the facts as they are in Heaven, we are getting access to the Mind of Christ. This is what we put our belief to, then we act on what we believe. When we are in FAITH we move and live from the place where what has been revealed to us has already happened in Heaven. We are just waiting for the manifestation on earth.

The spirit of fear is what Satan uses to get us to doubt the **Facts As In The Heavens (FAITH)** that is given to us by the Holy Spirit. This can hinder the manifestation process because our language is directly connected to what we believe. So, if we speak negative things toward what the Holy Spirit has shown us, it delays the manifestation process. Also, we can miss the manifestation of the promise if we are focused on the fear – **False Evidence Appearing Real** – that Satan presents to us. We are distracted by things that take our focus off God, which in turn causes us to not see what God has really done in our lives according to the kingdom of God.

When you are distracted, you begin to doubt and think God is not answering your prayers and your Faith becomes weaker and weaker. That is why this planner is so important. When these moments come, and we all have them, you have something tangible to reflect back on and remember what God has done, and he is Faithful to fulfill his promise.

This practice should not stop at the end of this planner. This should be an every day practice. The planner is to jumpstart this discipline in your life. You can use it to jumpstart your Faith journey, strengthen your

Faith journey, and when you are believing for something specific like healing, a job, transformed marriage or family member, etc. It is a great way to keep records of your Faith experiences with God. Sign up for the monthly subscription and you will receive a planner every month to document your Faith journey with God. This will assist you in flexing your Faith muscles as they get stronger in your walk with God in life.

THANK YOU

I pray this time and reflection of Faith has been insightful for you and has strengthened your trust in God. Do not stop FLEXING YOUR FAITH. If you want to pursue additional growth in developing your Faith and you would like to book a session, contact us at Ezekielfamilyservices.com, 240-244-0285, or ezekielfamilyservices@gmail.com. We specialize in Spirituotherapy which is a combination of therapy and biblical spiritual healing, and coaching, which moves you forward into the new goals you will create through your growth journey. Our social media platforms are Ezekiel Family Services (Facebook) and (Instagram).

"Flexing Your FAITH makes the impossible – POSSIBLE!"

ABOUT THE AUTHOR

NIKKI PINKNEY is a Minister of the gospel, Spirituotherapist, Certified International Coaching Federation Coach, Author, and Founder of Ezekiel Family Services. She lives a life of Faith and has believed God to heal her mentally, emotionally, physically, and spiritually. As a result of her Faith journey, she has a dynamic way of leading people into the awareness of the Holy Spirit's operation in their lives. Her passion is to help people see the workings of God in their lives. She is anointed to align people's minds to the mind of Christ! She enjoys coaching women and helping them get "unstuck" and experience breakthroughs, freedom, and alignment with their power and authority in Christ. Nikki has a way of helping women transform thinking patterns, own their power, overcome trauma, and embrace their unique beauty and giftings.

Nikki's Faith over the years has resulted in the healing power of God giving her a healthy marriage where she and her husband not only came to love each other but they like each other as well. This birthed into Nikki and her husband Jason the desire to coach pre-marital and married couples and they soon established a coaching practice, Ezekiel Family Services. Together their love for God and gratitude to him for his Faithfulness in healing their marriage propels them to empower couples with tools and strategies to create healthy and happy marriages.